Let's Go!
Animal Tracks
in the Snow!

Have Fun
Finding tracks!
Jime Poly

This book is dedicated
to my grandchildren,
Noah, Evan, Matthew, and Brianna.
May you always
see the world as you do now,
full of wonder and excitement.

ISBN 978-1-7320580-0-2 (hardcover)
ISBN 978-1-7320580-1-9 (softcover)

www.dianepolley.com

Let's Go! Animal Tracks in the Snow!

By Diane Polley

Illustrated by Marion Hall

Hooray! Hooray! It's a sunny day.
Let's get dressed
and go out to play.

Let's zip up our jackets,
put our hats on so tight.

Mittens to warm our hands—
now, we are all dressed just right.

But wait.
Look out the
window—what a sight.
Something happened
overnight!

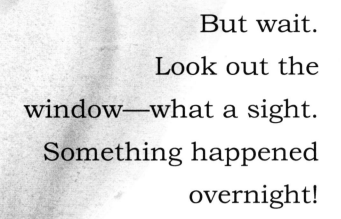

From the top of the trees
to way down below,
everything is covered
with a fresh blanket of snow!

Where do the animals go in the snow?
That is the question I'd like to know.
Let's explore with our eyes.
Let's look for their tracks.

Maybe they were here last night
looking for snacks.

Are the birds in the trees?

Did they fly down looking for treats?

Look!

Here, by the bird feeder,

can you hear their happy tweets?

The squirrels scurry
to and fro,
looking for acorns
in the snow.

Then back to their nests
in the trees
they will go!

Look!
Bunnies were here
going
hop,
hop,
hop!

Let's follow their tracks

to see where they stopped.

The fox is swift
  and clever,
    roaming at night

looking for a tasty morsel
  or just a quick bite.

His prey better hide
  and be quiet as a mouse.

Quick!
Scoot back into the
nooks and crannies
of our house!

The deer were here!
How do I know?
They left their tracks in the snow!

Hungry,
they explore at night,
looking for greens.
Returning to the woods
at daybreak,
hoping not to be seen.

Snow falls from the trees
with a great big

SPLATT!

Missy, our cat,
doesn't like that!

Rufus, our dog, likes to run and play.
His tracks in the snow
                    go
        every
                which
        way!

Our boots make tracks, too,
all over the snow.
Let's follow them back
to know where they go.
They lead us towards home;
that's where we should be.

So cozy and warm,
with cocoa and cake
for you
and for me!

Ready?
Set?
Go!!

Find these tracks
in the snow. . .

Songbirds have three toes pointed forward and one toe pointed backward. When a bird hops, the tracks are paired side by side. Look for this pattern in the snow for common tree-dwelling birds such as chickadees, cardinals, sparrows, and blue jays. Seeds dropped from a hanging feeder or berries from a bush will attract birds to fly down to the snow-covered ground.

Raccoon tracks can be found by water and may look like a child's tiny hand and foot prints. Also look for their tracks by overturned garbage pails or outdoor sources of food. If possible, before eating, a raccoon will dip his food into water, holding it delicately between his front paws. With mask like markings on their face, it's easy to see why raccoons are sometimes referred to as sneaky little bandits. Raccoons have five toes on both the front and back paws. The front toes are more "splayed" or spread apart than the rear toes. Raccoons press more weight onto their back paws so the heel may sink deeper into the snow, making it look longer and larger than the front print.

Squirrel tracks look like tiny hand prints in the snow. They walk in straight lines and sometimes you can see their claw marks at the end of their prints. They gather acorns and nuts in the fall to eat in the winter months. Look for their tracks around the bottom of tree trunks or under bird feeders, where they search for dropped seeds and nuts.

hipmunks are part of the squirrel family. They have four toes
1 the front paws and five on the back paws. Their tracks are
:ry similar to squirrels but are much smaller, making their claw
arks at the end of each track harder to see. Chipmunks are
ound dwellers, often making burrows in the ground, or in logs,
les of rocks, or stone walls. Their tracks may be less visible in
ie snow as they lie "torpid" or in semi-hibernation during the
Ider weather.

Rabbits "bound", or jump, rather than walk or run. Their small front paws touch the ground first, then their larger back paws ho over their front paws. This motion is very similar to children playing "leap frog." Look for these four tracks, a space, and then the next four tracks as they hop along their way. Wild rabbits live in the woods burrowing in the dirt for shelter and safety, but sometimes their tracks will lead you to temporary winter shelters under porches or sheds.

eer have hoofed toes which may look heart shaped in the snow. There will be two prints, side by side. If the snow is very deep you may see two small circles behind the larger hoof prints. Look for eer tracks entering open fields by exiting wooded areas or dense ndergrowth.

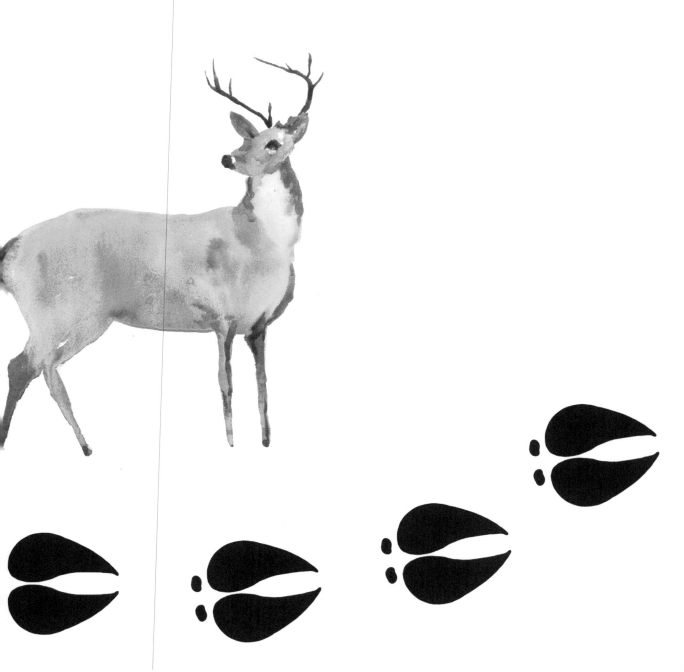

Foxes are straight-line walkers. They will place their rear foot in the same place their front foot walked. Their tracks are very similar to those of coyotes and domestic dogs. There will be four ovals (shaped liked arrow heads) and an upside-down heart shape perhaps with claw marks showing at the end of the toe tracks. You might spot their tracks following those tracks of a smaller prey such as a field mouse.

ommon field mouse tracks are very tiny and might be very hard
 spot in the snow. The tracks will have five toes on the hind
rints and four toes on the front prints. Mice need to be aware of
anger at all times so they move quickly over the snow, making
heir prints very shallow and light. Sometimes you will see a line
r "tail drag" after the prints. Look for tracks by the sides of sheds,
orches, or decks where mice may be seeking shelter for the
inter.

Cat tracks have a tear-drop shaped foot pad, with four toes on the front paws and four toes on the back paws. You might not see claw marks on the end of the toes since cats can "retract," or pull in, their claws when they want to. Cats walk in a straight-line pattern. Their tracks are similar to dog tracks but are usually much smaller. If you have outdoor cats, it is fun to follow their tracks out your door to see where they go.

Dogs are straight-line walkers. However, since dogs like to run in whatever direction they wish, you may see their footprints going in circles, or forward, then backwards again. Their footprints are larger than those of a cat and the footpad may look more triangular. You may also see claw marks at the end of the four toe prints. Unlike cats, dogs cannot retract their claws at will.

About the Author

Diane Polley resides in Essex, Massachusetts. She encouraged her three children, while growing up, to explore the outdoors from the woods to the nearby seashore. An avid walker, Diane finds the natural beauty of Cape Ann an inspiration for her children's stories. Sparking the imagination, her simple stories share ways to discover and respect our environment.

www.dianepolley.com

About the Illustrator

Marion Hall is an artist member of the Rockport Art Association, the North Shore Arts Association, and the New England Watercolor Society. She lives and teaches in Manchester, Massachusetts, and North Captiva, Florida.

www.marionhallwatercolorist.com

CPSIA information can be obtained
at www.ICGtesting.com
Printed in the USA
BVHW02n1718220818
524427BV00002B/4/P